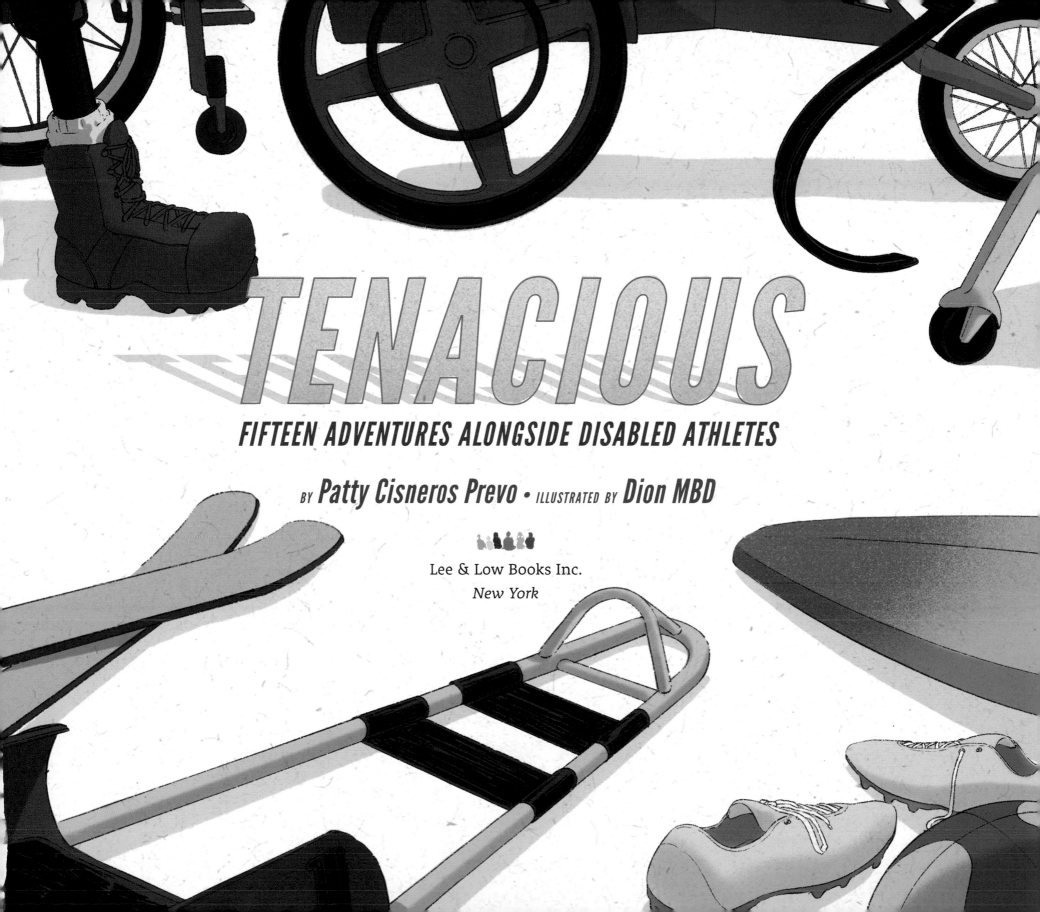

TENACIOUS

FIFTEEN ADVENTURES ALONGSIDE DISABLED ATHLETES

BY **Patty Cisneros Prevo** • ILLUSTRATED BY **Dion MBD**

Lee & Low Books Inc.
New York

Take a journey with this crew.
Come discover what they do!
Race and jump and shoot and soar
in sports events and so much more.
Passion is their common theme.
Have some fun and join the team!

One and two and step and turn! Be creative as you learn.

Doctors diagnosed **ANNABELLE GEIB** with spastic diplegia cerebral palsy when she was only a year old. Thanks to her physical therapy, dancing soon became a part of her life. Because adaptive dance lessons were hard to come by, she enrolled in nondisabled dance classes and learned to adapt the moves with the use of her leg braces and walker. Annabelle now performs tap, hip-hop, and ballet, and although she's usually the only kid with a disability at dance studios, her motto is "Whatever you can do, I can do." With her positive attitude and determination, she is also a motivational speaker and challenges others to take a chance and try something new.

Daily Challenge: "Navigating busy middle-school hallways when I'm not as steady as everyone else and can fall down easily, which is embarrassing."

Daily Joy: "TikTok dancing with my sister, Juliet!"

Pick up speed before the pit.

Then take your leap! And never quit.

JOHN REGISTER earned NCAA All-American honors in the long jump, high hurdles, and the 4 × 400-meter relay. While training for the 1996 Olympic trials in the hurdles, John hyperextended his left knee and severed an artery. The reconstruction of the artery failed, disease set in, and amputation of his left leg above the knee was the final result.

During his rehabilitation, John learned to walk with a prosthetic leg and discovered the Paralympic Games. In 1996 John made Team USA as a Paralympic swimmer, but his heart longed for the track. Four years later he won the Paralympic silver medal in long jump and set an American record. He says, "I did not overcome the loss of my limb. To overcome the loss would mean I'd have to grow it back. What I overcame were the limits I placed on myself and that others placed on me. This is what is universal for all of us to overcome."

Daily Challenge: "My daily challenge is staying inspired and motivated. And then trying to find that every single day."

Daily Joy: "My vision is to inspire by creating echo moments. Ripples go out—echoes come back. Echoes validate. When a person who has never met me comes up to me and says they heard my story through another medium and they acted to change their life because of it, I realize what I'm putting out is the right inspiration."

Shred across the alpine slopes.
Seize the mountain, filled with hopes.

When thirteen-year-old **DANELLE UMSTEAD** started experiencing poor vision and headaches, tests revealed retinitis pigmentosa, an eye disease that will eventually result in total blindness. After her dad became a guide for skiers with visual impairments, Danelle skied for the first time at age twenty-nine and found a life full of adventure, possibilities, and endless joy.

A few years later, Danelle met Rob Umstead on the slopes of New Mexico. Their chemistry was instant and in less than a year, they moved to Utah to ski and start a life together. Rob became Danelle's full-time guide, and their ski racing team, Vision4Gold, was born. In the middle of their career, doctors diagnosed Danelle with multiple sclerosis after she was experiencing stroke-like symptoms. Since then, Team Vision4Gold continued its focus and domination by winning more than fifty Alpine Skiing World Cup medals. Most recently, Danelle became the first blind/low vision contestant and third Paralympian on the television show *Dancing with the Stars*.

Daily Challenge: "It is really tough for me not to connect with people and family through simple gestures like a smile, or a wink, or holding up a hand to say hello. I would love to connect on a nonverbal basis, too, like to see my son smile at me or his emotions. I'm always having to ask."

Daily Joy: "Being blessed with an incredible husband who believes in me, challenges me, and, most of all, loves me unconditionally. When I am with him, I feel like anything is possible. That kind of love is hard to find."

Dribble, pass, and weave up court! Teammates need your full support.

Born with spina bifida, **CHRISTINA RIPP SCHWAB** always played alongside her nondisabled friends and often scooted around using her upper body when activities were not inclusive of wheelchair users. At age eleven Christina attended an Easter Seals camp and tried wheelchair basketball for the first time. With her incredible arm strength, she drained basket after basket.

Christina matured into a dominant athlete. She competed in five Paralympic Games in two different sports and came away with three gold medals in wheelchair basketball. She won eight National Wheelchair Basketball Association (NWBA) Championships and three MVP honors, and was inducted into the NWBA Hall of Fame. Christina also coached the US Men's Wheelchair Basketball Team to a gold medal at the 2020 Summer Paralympic Games as an assistant coach, and shortly after was named head coach to Team USA Women.

Daily Challenge: "Motherhood. Parenting is hard all around. My daily challenge is self-doubting, making sure I'm making the right choices for my boys, and questioning if I'm spending enough time with them."

Daily Joy: "Motherhood. My joy is coming home and seeing them. They're just so happy to see me. It makes my self-doubt melt away because they love me regardless."

Sprinting meters, set your pace!

Push yourself with pride and grace.

A car accident paralyzed seven-year-old **JESSICA GALLI CLOY** from the waist down. During her hospital stay, her recreational therapist suggested she try wheelchair racing. With specialized gloves and her feet tucked underneath the aerodynamic wheelchair, Jessica felt like she was soaring!

In a few years, she earned her first spot on the US Track and Field Team as a sprinter and went on to win seven Paralympic medals, including gold in the 400 meters. She also set world records in the 200-, 400-, and 800-meter sprints and was named the 2007 Paralympian of the Year. To give back, Jessica has stayed involved by coaching, volunteering, and working in the adaptive sports community.

Daily Challenge: "A daily challenge of mine is ensuring I live a balanced life so that I am able to give my best to my job, to spend quality time with my family, and to find time to do the things I truly enjoy. Life can feel busy at times and there are days where I feel like I've lost myself. My goal each day is to stay centered, remember what's most important to me, and strive for happiness wherever it can be found."

Daily Joy: "A daily joy is putting my daughters to bed. While we are all often exhausted and cranky by bedtime, I really enjoy getting some quiet time with each of my daughters to read with them and wish them good dreams."

Balance, kick, attack upfield.

Goals and strengths will be revealed.

ELI WOLFF survived a stroke at two years old, resulting in impairments in his left arm and leg. As a kid, he was interested in soccer and played throughout high school and college. While a student-athlete at Brown University, Eli took a course on sports and society. He wondered why there was no mention of disability in the course, and so a passion was born: the fight for inclusion in sport for *all* people.

Eli played on the US Paralympic Soccer Team for almost ten years, but more importantly, he used his experiences to advocate for the dignity of and respect for people with disabilities. Among other actions, he organized support for golfer Casey Martin, who sued the Professional Golfers Association (PGA) for the right to use a golf cart for his circulatory condition—and won! Eli is now the co-director of Disability in Sport International, advancing education, advocacy, and research for inclusion in sports.

Daily Challenge: "Staying patient and understanding. As an educator and advocate, I have to recognize the speed of change can be slow and steady and occasionally quick and rapid."

Daily Joy: "Time with my kids, Stella and Spencer, and my partner, Cheri. I really love time with family to relax and regroup. I feel so lucky to be a parent and am always learning and adapting as a husband and a parent of two little ones."

Doin' great!

At 6'3" and with severe osteoarthritis, **DR. ANDREA WOODSON-SMITH** towered and powered over her opponents in both able-bodied and wheelchair basketball. While training for the Paralympic Games, Andrea stumbled upon CrossFit, a strength and conditioning program. She loved the intensity and speed of the workouts, which she could do from her sports chair. "You go into the box and bang some weights and turn into the beast you imagine yourself to be!"

Andrea started competing in adaptive CrossFit after the Paralympic Games and took first place at the CrossFit Exchange Competition. She also won back-to-back first-place finishes in Adaptive CrossFit at the Working Wounded Games.

Daily Challenge: "My daily challenge has been finding the balance between parenting and work. I'm having to work from home and help with school. It has been a huge challenge."

Daily Joy: "My daily joy is when I have these long days out and about and being able to spend that time with my sons. We can spend the majority of the day together, which is not typical of teenagers."

Swing and hit and catch and throw.

Curveballs help you learn and grow.

Doctors diagnosed **DAN FERREIRA** at birth with osteogenesis imperfecta, a disease that makes one's bones brittle. Introduced to wheelchair basketball in his early teens, Dan played and coached the sport at every level for more than thirty years. Wheelchair basketball can be very physical, so his longevity in the sport was quite a feat for someone vulnerable to broken bones. When he took a liking to wheelchair softball, he quickly established himself as a competitive player and coach once again.

Dan won multiple championships, facilitated grassroots programs, and received numerous recognitions in wheelchair softball including the National Wheelchair Softball Association Award for his leadership. The lifelong coach says, "Adaptive sport is more than fun. It is an empowering space that every kid with a physical disability deserves."

Daily Challenge: "A daily challenge is educating the world on stereotypes about people with disabilities. I'm not everyone's hero. I'm just a good dad and a good husband, and I want to take care of my family."

Daily Joy: "My daily joy is getting up and seeing my family every morning. That's my beginning and end every day. I want to be a good dad and husband for them."

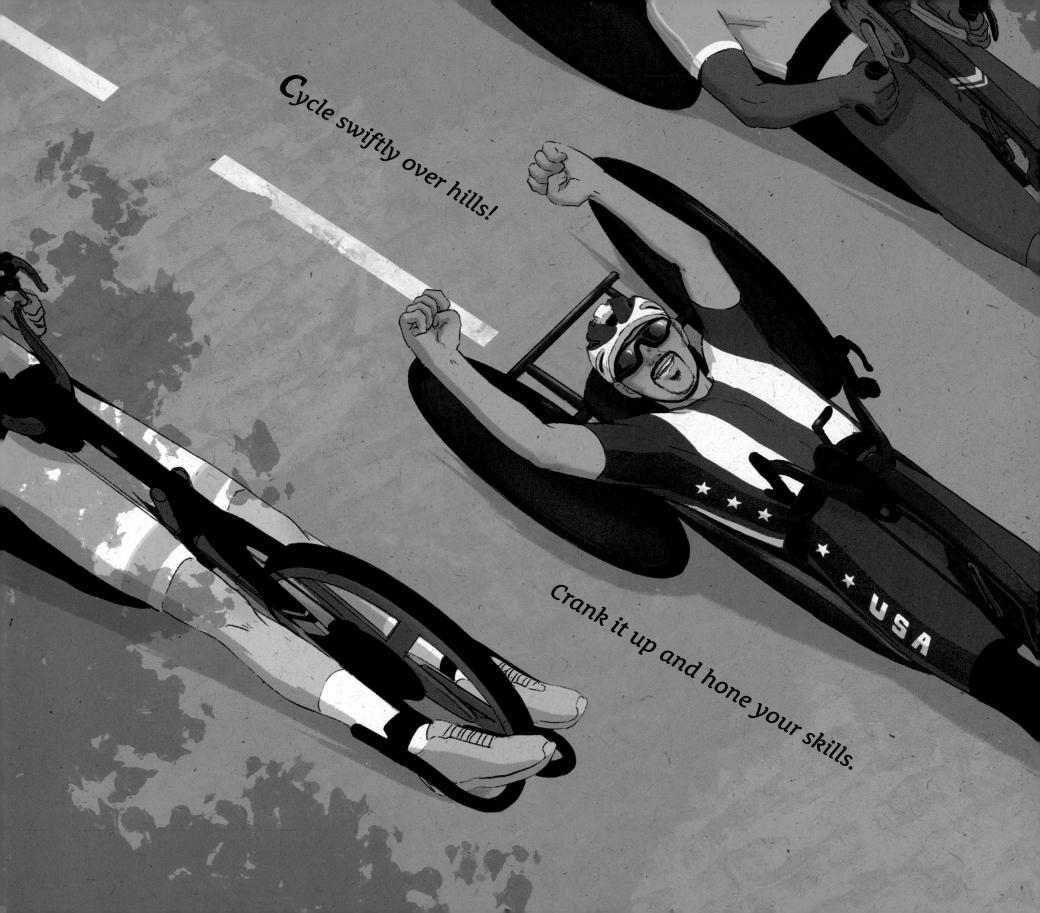

Cycle swiftly over hills!

Crank it up and hone your skills.

At age twenty-six, **WILL GROULX** was involved in a motorcycle crash resulting in a spinal cord injury. The former collegiate volleyball player and US Navy sailor became paralyzed from the chest down, and he struggled with the transition to his new life as a quadriplegic. Wheelchair rugby helped him hammer out his frustrations and adjust to his disability.

After competing in rugby at the Paralympic level, Will switched to road cycling and exchanged his armored rugby chair for an aerodynamic recumbent handcycle. He won three World Championship cycling titles, earned more than thirty World Cup podium finishes, and has been nominated twice for an ESPN ESPY (Excellence in Sports Performance Yearly) Award in the category of Best Male Athlete with a Disability.

Daily Challenge: "Trying to explain to someone how to carry, repair, or move something that I could have easily done myself before my accident. It's an incredibly frustrating exercise in patience."

Daily Joy: "I take great joy when either of my kids ask me to do anything with them: ride a bike, read a book, play a game, etc. I know the time is coming as they grow up when their parents will embarrass them, so I'll take every minute I can get right now."

Wheels in motion. Racket set.

Mental toughness at the net.

In her twenties, **HOPE LEWELLEN** worked as an aircraft mechanic. One day when she was assisting in moving an airplane to the terminal, the nose wheel of the plane caught Hope's legs. Her right leg had to be amputated above the knee.

She dabbled in wheelchair basketball during her rehab, and teammates encouraged Hope to try other adaptive sports. Because of her mental toughness and quickness in a sports chair, tennis was a great fit. In just a couple of years, Hope made her first US Wheelchair Tennis Team and won the Paralympic silver medal in tennis doubles. After more than two decades on the wheelchair tennis circuit, and also winning two Paralympic medals in the sport of sitting volleyball, Hope now mentors other LGBTQ+ athletes in embracing their identities on and off the court.

Daily Challenge: "A daily challenge is having patience in a world not designed or intended for disabled people."

Daily Joy: "One of the best times in my day is playing with my dogs and just feeling the joy they get from the littlest things."

Sled secured to take the ice.

Rip the shot. Don't think twice!

RICO ROMAN joined the US Army after high school. During his third tour in Iraq, Rico's Humvee hit an improvised explosive device (IED), and the blast led to the amputation of his left leg above the knee. During his rehab, a group called Operation Comfort introduced him to sled hockey. Athletes sit on sleds with hockey blades attached underneath and maneuver across the ice using specialized sticks.

Rico came to love the speed, the intensity, and particularly the brotherhood of the sport. In 2014, 2018, and 2022 Rico and the US Sled Hockey Team won back-to-back Paralympic gold medals. He encourages young disabled athletes to try a number of sports, saying, "There's something out there for everybody. Find something you can do and don't focus on what you can't do. Get it!"

Daily Challenge: "Not talking myself out of a workout."

Daily Joy: "My little Peanut, my wiener dog, AKA Peanut Butter!"

Journey upward, climb the peak. Reach the heights you dare to seek.

After **SANDY DUKAT** was born with an underdeveloped leg, her parents and doctors decided to amputate the limb to give her greater mobility and a more active life. She soon blossomed into an incredible athlete, eventually setting a world record in the marathon for women with above-the-knee amputations.

After years of competing in ski racing at the Paralympic level, Sandy teamed up with other disabled women to climb Mount Kilimanjaro, the highest peak in Africa. As an athlete who thrived on adrenaline and mental preparation, Sandy later trekked up Cayambe and Cotopaxi, two of the highest volcanos in Ecuador, to raise awareness and funds for those living with limb loss in developing countries.

Daily Challenge: "Reminding onlookers that I am strong, independent, and capable."

Daily Joy: "Whether it is on the slopes, in the skate park, or just in our backyard, I have the ability and mobility to be active with my son."

Paddle farther, surf the wave.

Trust yourself. Be bold! Be brave!

MEIRA VA'A NELSON grew up on Western Samoa, an island in the Pacific Ocean. As an islander, she loved to swim, fish, and pick clams and oysters, and she developed an unbreakable bond with the ocean. When an accident partially paralyzed her at age fourteen, Meira discovered adaptive surfing. She strapped herself into a waveski—an adapted surf kayak—and used a paddle to balance and navigate the waves. Meira soon won multiple awards in the sport, including first place at the 2018 US Open Adaptive Surfing Championships. Most recently, she won the 2022 Hawaii Adaptive Surfing Championship and 2022 Association of Adaptive Surfing Professionals (AASP) World Championship Tour.

Daily Challenge: "After the passing of my daughter, I felt an immense feeling of failure. I felt like I had failed at parenting in the sense of not doing the right thing, not being enough for my kids and for my loved ones. I put a lot of pressure on myself more than ever after her passing to do everything right, and it's extremely exhausting."

Daily Joy: "My family! At the end of the day, when they go to bed happy, I'm happy. I find joy in their laughs and smiles, when we sit at the table and eat dinner, and when we tell funny stories."

Camp out under starry nights.

Find your fire, set your sights.

At thirteen years old, **EVE HAMPTON** woke up one morning and struggled to walk. Within minutes of arriving at the hospital, she was paralyzed. Eve had contracted transverse myelitis, a rare spinal cord disease. Frustrated and confused, she sought peace and healing in the great outdoors. She navigated trails using a wheelchair attachment designed to traverse rough terrain and sought out campgrounds that offered wheelchair-accessible tables and elevated campsites for easier transfers from her wheelchair. One year, Eve camped and hiked in twelve national parks in a single summer. She says, "Adversity is like a blockade in the path. Instead of being stopped, use the obstacle as a moment to pause. Look around and see where else you might venture forth."

Daily Challenge: "Between packing snacks, wrangling kids into car seats, and making sure everyone has their rain boots on the right feet, just getting out of the house is a daily challenge."

Daily Joy: "Getting outdoors with kids forces you to slow down. I love watching the seasons change with them. Assessing the color of a fallen leaf, finding footprints in the snow, watching the path of a ladybug . . . ordinary things become moments of wonder."

Drop in, pop it, grind the rail. Take a risk! Let skills prevail.

DELMACE MAYO was born in Haiti and sustained an unknown spinal cord injury. Adopted as a toddler, Delmace transitioned into his new life in the US and tried sled hockey, wheelchair basketball, and other adaptive sports. One day he saw a billboard for the Nitro Circus, an event headlining athletes in BMX, skate, and other action sports. Aaron "Wheelz" Fotheringham was featured along with his specialized wheelchair. Fascinated, Delmace researched Aaron and his sport—wheelchair motocross (WCMX)—and registered for his first WCMX clinic days later. By the age of thirteen Delmace became a three-time WCMX Champion, and he hopes to see the sport included in future Paralympic Games. Delmace continues to compete in other sports and recently won seven gold medals at the Move United Junior Track & Field Nationals. He has been named a Boston Public Schools Male Track Athlete of the Year and Youth Male Athlete of the Year by the National Congress of State Games.

Daily Challenge: "Getting up early to get to school on time."

Daily Joy: "Having TV time with my mom at night."

Strong, determined, all with grit! You're tenacious! GO FOR IT!

Author's Note

At age eighteen I became a part of the wonderful community of disabled people. As a freshman at Indiana University, I was involved in a car accident resulting in a spinal cord injury. During rehab, my physical therapist introduced me to wheelchair basketball, and as an avid athlete, I was hooked. It was so much more than a sport. It was therapeutic emotionally, mentally, and physically. I was surrounded by individuals who had goals and dreams. As a young disabled adult, that's what I needed in order to push forward. I went on to compete at the 2000, 2004, and 2008 Paralympic Games and win back-to-back gold medals—one as captain at the 2008 Beijing Paralympic Games.

When I began writing *Tenacious*, I wanted to showcase the rich diversity in the adaptive sports world. And luckily, through the power of sport and community, I consider all the featured athletes in this book to be close friends. They each graciously made themselves available to be interviewed and answered all my questions. I am grateful to know and share their stories. All fifteen of these individuals agree that their own *tenacious* journey toward a full, meaningful life began with the support of family, friends, and the vast, encouraging community of disabled people. If you or someone you know has acquired a disability and needs support—whether disability-related or sport-related—please visit the resources listed here or on my website, pattycisnerosprevo.com.

Photo courtesy @ Tillie Vuksich DBA TAV Media Company

Daily Challenge: As a disabled athlete, I have often engaged in and perpetuated ableist language and culture. The activist Talila "TL" Lewis defines ableism as "a system of assigning value to people's bodies and minds based on societally constructed ideas of normalcy, productivity, desirability, intelligence, excellence, and fitness." Simply put, ableism is a system of oppression that discriminates or is prejudiced against disabled people. One of the most common and harmful tropes of ableist culture is the "supercrip" trope. Disabled people are portrayed as somehow "overcoming" or "fixing" their disability through some superhuman effort or other ability, and not because we are driven, passionate, and tenacious people. I am constantly challenged to recognize my own internalized ableism and learn how to become a better disability advocate.

Daily Joy: Spending as much free time as I can with my two amazing kids, Elliana and Elliot.

Preferred Language in This Book

As an advocate in this space who continues to learn more about the disability justice movement, I prefer using identity-first language versus person-first language. Identity-first language puts the disability before the person, like "disabled girl." Person-first language puts the person before the disability, like "girl with a disability." As the author of *Tenacious*, it was a personal decision to mostly use identity-first language. It is important to note, however, that it is always best to ask individuals how they prefer to identify.

Here are some other terms to consider while discussing this book:

Instead of *disAbled, differently abled, physically challenged . . .*
Use **disabled** or **disability**.
Disabled and *disability* are not bad words. Having a disability or being disabled is a culture and identity.
I am disabled. I have a disability.

Instead of *handicapped . . .* Use **accessible**.
Language is constantly changing, and *handicapped* is outdated.
They are parked in an accessible parking spot. She is using the accessible bathroom stall.

Instead of *use your voice . . .* Use **platform**.
Not everyone has spoken language.
The activist used his platform.

Instead of *wheelchair-bound . . .* Use **wheelchair user**.
Disabled people can move in and out of their wheelchairs. They are not stuck to them.
The kid is a wheelchair user.

Instead of *special needs . . .* Use **needs**.
We all have needs. Disabled people have needs, and their needs are not special because the person is disabled.
The student was given extra time for the test to better meet her needs.

Resources

Accessibility in the National Parks
https://www.nps.gov/aboutus/accessibility.htm

Americans with Disabilities Act
https://www.ada.gov

Association of Adaptive Surfing Professionals
https://adaptivesurfingprofessionals.com/

CrossFit Games Adaptive Divisions 2022
https://games.crossfit.com/article/2022-crossfit-games-season-adaptive-divisions/games

International Paralympic Committee
https://www.paralympic.org

Move United
https://moveunitedsport.org/

National Wheelchair Basketball Association (NWBA)
https://www.nwba.org/

National Wheelchair Softball Association (NWSA)
https://www.wheelchairsoftball.org/

Operation Comfort
https://operationcomfort.org/

US Department of Veterans Affairs
https://www.va.gov

US Paralympics
https://www.teamusa.org/Team-USA-Athlete-Services/Paralympic-Sport-Development

US Tennis Association (USTA) Wheelchair Tennis
https://www.usta.com/en/home/play/adult-tennis/programs/national/about-wheelchair-tennis.html

Wheelchair Motocross (WCMX) International
https://wcmxinternational.com/

Glossary

Adaptive *adjective* adapted or changed to help individuals

Advocate *noun* someone who strongly supports and fights for a cause

Aerodynamic *adjective* specifically designed to go fast

Amputate *verb* to surgically remove a part of the body

Artery *noun* a vessel carrying blood from the heart to the rest of the body

Cerebral palsy *noun* a condition caused by damage to the brain before birth resulting in impairments

Disability *noun* a condition that impairs a part or parts of the body

Disability justice *noun* a movement that centers the intersection of disability and other underrepresented identities like race, sexual orientation, gender identity, etc.

Handcycle *noun* an adaptive cycle powered by the use of the arms and not the legs

Impairment *noun* a lack of movement or function

LGBTQ+ *noun* lesbian, gay, bisexual, transgender, queer, plus

Limb *noun* a body part like an arm or a leg

Multiple sclerosis (MS) *noun* a condition that impairs the central nervous system

Osteoarthritis *noun* a condition in which the cartilage between bones wears down and causes pain

Osteogenesis imperfecta (OI) *noun* a disease that causes weak bones to break easily

Paralympic Games *noun* an elite sport competition for people with disabilities

Paralyzed *adjective* not able to move a part or parts of the body

Prosthetic *noun* an artificial body part

Quadriplegic *noun* a person completely or incompletely paralyzed from the chest down

Rehabilitation (rehab) *noun* care or therapy with the goal of getting back to better health

Retinitis pigmentosa *noun* an eye disease that affects the retina, causing a loss of vision

Spina bifida *noun* a condition caused by the underdevelopment of the spine and spinal cord before birth

Spinal cord injury (SCI) *noun* damage to the spinal cord often causing paralysis

Stroke *noun* a medical condition that occurs when blood vessels carrying oxygen to the brain are blocked or stopped

Transverse myelitis (TM) *noun* a disease caused by inflammation of the spinal cord

Visual impairment *noun* a condition such as low vision, partial vision, or blindness

Wheelchair *noun* a chair with wheels to assist with mobility needs

A Timeline of the Paralympics

1944: Near the end of World War II, Dr. Ludwig Guttmann opened a spinal injuries center at the Stoke Mandeville Hospital in Great Britain for returning war veterans and civilians. He provided sports as a way of mental, physical, and social rehab for wheelchair patients.

1948: During the London Olympic Games, Dr. Guttmann organized an archery competition in which wheelchair athletes—fourteen men and two women—competed as the first Paralympians. This event was named the Stoke Mandeville Games and was meant to coincide with the Olympic Games.

1952: The Stoke Mandeville Games became an international competition when the Netherlands sent athletes to compete.

1960: The Stoke Mandeville Games officially became the first Paralympic Games in Rome, Italy. There were four hundred athletes from twenty-three countries. The Paralympic Games were then held every four years like the Olympics.

1976: Örnsköldsvik, Sweden, hosted the first Winter Paralympic Games. There were 198 athletes from sixteen countries.

1988: The Summer Paralympic Games were held for the first time in the same city—Seoul, South Korea—using the same venues as the Summer Olympic Games.

1989: The International Paralympic Committee (IPC) was founded. The IPC and the International Olympic Committee agreed to have the Paralympic Games take place in the same cities and venues as the Olympic Games.

1992: The Winter Paralympic Games were held for the first time in the same city—Albertville, France—using the same venues as the Winter Olympic Games.

The Paralympic Games have certainly grown! Most recently, the 2020 Summer Paralympic Games—which were postponed to 2021 due to the global pandemic—welcomed around 4400 athletes from 162 national Paralympic committees and held 539 medal events in Tokyo, Japan. The 2022 Winter Paralympic Games, hosted in Beijing, China, featured around 564 athletes from 46 national Paralympic committees and held 78 medal events.

To Dow, thanks for being my rookie mistake and leading me in the right direction.
To Tony, Elliana, Elliot, and Bella (RIP), thank you for ALL the read-alouds.
Love you with my whole heart & soul.
—P.C.P.

To Fanny, for seeing me as me beyond anything that is visible.
To my parents, for believing in me having a visual career despite my eyes' condition.
—D. MBD

Bibliography

Disability and Philanthropy Forum. "What Is Disability Justice?" Accessed October 5, 2022. https://disabilityphilanthropy.org/resource/what-is-disability-justice/

Inside the Games. "The History of the Paralympic Movement." Accessed October 5, 2022. https://www.insidethegames.biz/articles/1010776/the-history-of-the-paralympic-movement

International Paralympic Committee. "Paralympics History." Accessed October 5, 2022. https://www.paralympic.org/ipc/history

Lewis, Talila A. "Working Definition of Ableism: January 2022 Update." January 1, 2022. https://www.talilalewis.com/blog/working-definition-of-ableism-january-2022-update

PBS. "About the Paralympics: Paralympic History." Accessed October 5, 2022. https://www.pbs.org/wgbh/medal-quest/past-games/

Toole, Tucker C. "How the Paralympic Movement Evolved into a Major Sporting Event." *National Geographic*, September 2, 2021. https://www.nationalgeographic.com/history/article/how-the-paralympic-movement-evolved-into-major-sporting-event

Treisman, Rachel. "When Did the Paralympics Start? Here's a Brief History of the Games." NPR, August 25, 2021. https://www.npr.org/2021/08/25/1030629549/paralympics-history-name-meaning

Text copyright © 2023 by Patty Cisneros Prevo
Illustrations copyright © 2023 by Dion MBD
All rights reserved. No part of this book may be reproduced, transmitted, or stored in an information retrieval system in any form or by any means, electronic, mechanical, photocopying, recording, or otherwise, without written permission from the publisher.
LEE & LOW BOOKS Inc., 95 Madison Avenue, New York, NY 10016
leeandlow.com
Edited by Cheryl Klein
Book design by Christy Hale
Book production by The Kids at Our House
The text is set in Rooney
Manufactured in China by RR Donnelley
First Edition
10 9 8 7 6 5 4 3 2 1
Cataloging-in-Publication data is available at the Library of Congress
ISBN 9781643790985 (hc) ISBN 9781643796550 (ebk)